Biblical Fou

Building
for Eternity

by Larry Kreider

House To House Publications
Ephrata, Pennsylvania USA

Building for Eternity

Larry Kreider

Updated Edition © 2002, Reprinted 2003
Copyright © 1993, 1997, 1999
House to House Publications
1924 West Main Street, Ephrata, PA 17522
Telephone: (717) 738-3751
FAX: (717) 738-0656
Web site: www.dcfi.org

ISBN 1-886973-03-2
Design and illustrations by Sarah Mohler

CONTENTS

Books in this Series

This is the fourth book in a twelve-book series designed to help believers to build a solid biblical foundation in their lives.

1 **Knowing Jesus Christ as Lord**
God's purpose for our lives through a personal relationship with Jesus

2 **The New Way of Living**
True repentance and faith toward God

3 **New Testament Baptisms**
Four baptisms including baptism in water and baptism in the Holy Spirit

4 **Building For Eternity**
The hope of the resurrection, the laying on of hands and eternal judgment

5 **Living in the Grace of God**
Applying God's grace to everyday living

6 **Freedom from the Curse**
Christ brings freedom to every area of our lives

7 **Learning to Fellowship with God**
How to deepen our relationship with Jesus Christ

8 **What is the Church?**
Finding our place in God's family

9 **Authority and Accountability**
How to respond to leadership and fellow believers God places in our lives

10 **God's Perspective on Finances**
How God wants His people to handle money

11 **Called to Minister**
Every Christian's call to serve

12 **The Great Commission**
Our purpose for living on this planet

A corresponding *Biblical Foundations for Children* book is also available (see page 63).

Introduction

The foundation of the Christian faith is built on Jesus Christ and His Word to us, the Holy Bible. This twelve-book *Biblical Foundation Series* includes elementary principles every Christian needs to help lay a strong spiritual foundation in his or her life. In this fourth Biblical Foundation book, *Building For Eternity,* we look at the final three of the six foundational doctrines of the Christian faith found in Hebrews 6:1-2—**the laying on of hands, the resurrection of the dead and eternal judgment:** *Therefore, leaving the discussion of the elementary principles of Christ, let us go on to perfection, not laying again the foundation of repentance from dead works and of faith toward God, of the doctrine of baptisms, of laying on of hands, of resurrection of the dead, and of eternal judgment (NKJ).* The foundational doctrine of the laying on of hands is an act in which one person imparts or conveys blessing, healing and/or authority to another for a specific spiritual purpose. We will learn that the laying on of hands has a vital connection with many aspects of our Christian lives. The hope of the resurrection is another biblical foundation that is so important to a Christian's faith because those who believe in Christ will share in His resurrection and have eternal life! Another foundation stone that is linked to the resurrection of the dead is eternal judgment. Every man and woman who has ever lived will be judged by God for all of eternity. The reality of an eternal judgment should cause all believers to hate sin and diligently seek the lost to tell them of God's wonderful plan for mankind!

In this book, the foundation truths from the Word of God are presented with modern day parables that help you easily understand the basics of Christianity. Use this book and the other 11 *Biblical Foundation* books to lay a solid spiritual foundation in your life, or if you are already a mature Christian, these books are great tools to assist you in discipling others. May His Word become life to you today.

God bless you!

Larry Kreider

How to Use This Resource

Personal study

Read from start to finish as an individual study program to build a firm Christian foundation and develop spiritual maturity.

- Each chapter has a key verse excellent to commit to memory.
- Additional scriptures in gray boxes are used for further study.
- Each reading includes questions for personal reflection and room to journal at the end of the book.

Daily devotional

Use as a devotional for a daily study of God's Word.

- Each chapter is divided into 7-day sections for weekly use.
- Additional days at the end of the book bring the total number of devotionals to one complete month. The complete set of 12 books gives one year's worth of daily devotionals.
- Additional scriptures are used for further study.
- Each day includes reflection questions and a place to write answers at the end of the book.

Mentoring relationship

Use for a spiritual parenting relationship to study, pray and discuss life applications together.

- A spiritual father or mother can easily take a spiritual son or daughter through these short Bible study lessons and use the reflection questions to provoke dialogue about what is learned.
- Read each day or an entire chapter at a time.

Small group study

Study this important biblical foundation in a small group setting.

- The teacher studies the material in the chapters and teaches, using the user-friendly outline provided at the end of the book.

Taught as a biblical foundation course

These teachings can be taught by a pastor or other Christian leader as a basic biblical foundation course.

- Students read an assigned portion of the material.
- In the class, the leader teaches the assigned material using the chapter outlines at the end of the book.

CHAPTER 1

Imparting
Blessing and Healing

KEY MEMORY VERSE

For this reason I remind you to fan into
flame the gift of God, which is in you
through the laying on of my hands.
2 Timothy 1:6

An elementary principle:
The laying on of hands

A few years ago, I visited a Bible School where I met an elderly gentleman. He had experienced God moving in miraculous ways during his lifetime, and I asked him if he would be willing to come to my dormitory room to pray for me. I knew that he had something I needed. As he laid his hands on me and prayed, I sensed the Lord giving me His blessing through this precious man of God. I knew that according to the scriptures, something happens when one believer lays his hands on another believer and prays for him. He *gives* or *imparts* something, through his teaching or influence, that the other person needs.

In Leviticus 16:21-22, Aaron laid his hands on a live goat and confessed the people's sins which were imparted from his hands to the goat. This supernatural transference happened through the laying on of hands.

What happens in this supernatural transference? The Bible tells us there is a clear impartation of power and God's blessing that is transferred from one person to another through the laying on of hands. "The laying on of hands" is another one of the important foundation stones that we need to place in our Christian lives from Hebrews 6:1-2. *Therefore, leaving the discussion of the elementary principles of Christ, let us go on to perfection, not laying again the foundation of...the laying on of hands...(NKJ)*

The Lord's purpose for the foundation stone of *the laying on of hands* is for us to experience the Lord's blessing and to be a blessing to others. In the Old Testament, the laying on of hands was an accepted practice for imparting blessing to be transmitted to future generations. Jacob imparted the blessing of God to his children by laying hands on them before he died (Genesis 48:14).

A friend of mine tells the true story of a Christian man who realized that he was close to the end of his life and was soon going to go to be with his Father in Heaven. He gathered his children around and imparted God's blessings to each of them. He then

REFLECTION
What is supernatural about the laying on of hands? Have you ever asked another Christian to impart a blessing to you by the laying on of hands? Describe what you asked for.

went into his bedroom, lay down and went home to be with the Lord. This is a true, modern-day example of imparting the blessing of God.

We don't have to wait until we come to the end of our lives to impart our blessing through the laying on of hands, however! In the next two chapters, we will examine how *the laying on of hands* is for imparting not only blessing, but also healing, spiritual gifts and authority.

Imparting life to one another

There is a tremendous power in our lives to bless, encourage and help people just by touching them. I believe this especially applies to children. Those who serve in a children's nursery are able to bless children by holding them in their arms and speaking God's Word over them. One night there was a child in our home who continued to cry. I took the crying child in my arms and prayed in the Spirit as I imparted the blessing of God to him. After a few minutes, the child became peaceful. What a privilege it was to impart a spiritual blessing of peace to that child. Jesus Himself did this. *And he took the children in his arms, put his hands on them and blessed them (Mark 10:16).* I lay my hands on my children each night before they go to bed. As I pray for them, I am imparting the Lord's health, healing, grace, and anointing into their lives. Why? Because there is power released as we impart spiritual blessings to others.

I love to shake people's hands for the first time. As a believer in Jesus Christ, we can shake someone's hand and impart, through a type of laying on of hands, faith, conviction, the grace of God, and the Lord's anointing into their lives. The Lord wants us to be a blessing to others so we may inherit a blessing from Him according to 1 Peter 3:8-9. *Finally, all of you, live in harmony with one another; be sympathetic, love as brothers, be compassionate and humble. Do not repay evil with evil or insult with insult, but with blessing, because to this you were called so that you may inherit a blessing.*

REFLECTION
How does the Lord impart a blessing to us and through us?

Something supernatural happens when we understand the principle of the laying on of hands and participate in this life-giving truth. When Spirit-filled Christians lay their hands on others and pray a prayer of faith, the power of God that is in them will also be received by the person for whom they are praying. Did you ever hug someone who had strong perfume on, and then for the next few minutes, you continue to smell that perfume or cologne? When someone lays their hands on you, they impart to you something that the Lord has given them. Something that is on them gets on you. We can lay our hands on others and impart the blessings of God to them and they can do the same for us.

Imparting the power of the Holy Spirit

DAY 3

In both the Old and New Testament, there are numerous examples of the laying on of hands, where one person laid hands on another person for a very specific purpose. Let's take a few moments and look at some distinct purposes that we see in the scriptures for the laying on of hands. Notice first of all how the power of the Holy Spirit is imparted through the laying on of hands. In Acts 8:14-15;17, we observe that the laying on of hands helped those who were seeking the baptism in the Holy Spirit. *When the apostles in Jerusalem heard that Samaria had accepted the word of God, they sent Peter and John to them. When they arrived, they prayed for them that they might receive the Holy Spirit...Then Peter and John placed their hands on them, and they received the Holy Spirit.*

Peter and John went down to Samaria, laid their hands on the new believers and they received the baptism in the Holy Spirit. You may ask, "Must I have someone lay hands on me to be baptized with the Holy Spirit?" No, you don't have to. However, something supernatural happens when a Spirit-filled believer in Jesus Christ lays hands on another person and prays a prayer of faith. God supernaturally works through His people and gives them the divine ability to impart the mighty power of the Holy Spirit as they pray in faith.

REFLECTION
Can you receive the Holy Spirit without the laying on of hands? Has God used you to impart the Holy Spirit to someone through the laying on of hands? Describe.

Many years ago, a friend laid his hands on me and prayed, and I began to pray in a new language. (I spoke in tongues.) Now I have the same privilege of laying hands on people and seeing them baptized with the Holy Spirit and praying in tongues. And so do you. The laying on of hands to impart the baptism in the Holy Spirit is not just for the believers in the book of Acts, it is also true for us today.

Jesus Christ is the same yesterday, today, and forever (Hebrews 13:8). He desires to use you to pray for others to be baptized in the Holy Spirit as you lay your hands on them and pray a prayer of faith. Expect the Lord to use you!

Imparting spiritual gifts

Another purpose for the laying on of hands is for the imparting of spiritual gifts. Paul said in Romans 1:11-12 that he wanted to impart spiritual gifts to them so they would be strengthened in their faith. *I long to see you so that I may impart to you some spiritual gift to make you strong—that is, that you and I may be mutually encouraged by each other's faith.*

Jesus wants us to not only impart the baptism in the Holy Spirit through the laying on of hands, but also to impart spiritual gifts that the Holy Spirit gives. 1 Corinthians 12:8-10 speaks of nine of these supernatural spiritual gifts. *To one there is given through the Spirit the message of wisdom, to another the message of knowledge by means of the same Spirit, to another faith by the same Spirit, to another gifts of healing by that one Spirit, to another miraculous powers, to another prophecy, to another distinguishing between spirits, to another speaking in different kinds of tongues, and to still another the interpretation of tongues.*

As we receive particular spiritual gifts from the Lord and learn how to use and exercise them, we can then lay hands on others and impart these gifts to them. These are not the only gifts the Holy Spirit gives to the body of Christ to be used among His people. Other gifts mentioned in Romans 12:6-8 are the gifts of prophecy, serving, teaching, encouraging, giving, leading, and mercy. These gifts are inward desires or motivations we have that enable us to build up God's people and express His love to others.

There are many supernatural and very practical spiritual gifts that God gives us. When God gives them to us, He then gives us the power and ability to lay our hands on others so they also can see these gifts begin to blossom in their own lives. The Lord wants to use you to impart to others what He has given you.

Maybe you need *discernment* or a *gift of faith*. Find someone who has this gift operating in his or her life. Ask him or her to lay hands on you and pray for you. Many times I have asked others to lay their hands on me and pray for me, and I have received supernatural ability and spiritual strength. Other times I have had the privilege of laying my hands on others and imparting a gift of faith, and they received spiritual strength and a renewed faith.

REFLECTION
List the nine spiritual gifts found in 1 Corinthians 12. List seven more spiritual gifts found in Romans 12. Do you have any of these gifts? Have you imparted any of them to others?

DAY 5

Associate with those who can impart gifts to you

The anointing and gifts of God are enhanced by associating with people who have these kinds of gifts operating in their lives. This gives us a greater opportunity to get these gifts transferred or imparted to us. When we rub shoulders with those who have certain spiritual gifts, they can lay their hands on us to impart that gift to us. In 1 Timothy 4:14, Paul said, *Do not neglect your gift, which was given you through a prophetic message when the body of elders laid their hands on you.*

The leaders of the church laid their hands on Timothy, and God gave him the spiritual gifts that he needed to fulfill his responsibilities. Paul told Timothy to not neglect the gifts he had received from the Lord through the laying on of hands. He also told Timothy that he needs to stir up these gifts. *For this reason I remind you to fan into flame the gift of God, which is in you through the laying on of my hands (2 Timothy 1:6).*

If you have the gift of prophecy, or the gift of serving or the gift of mercy, you can stir up these gifts as you pray in the Spirit and exercise these gifts. As you confess the truth of the Word of God, and thank God that He has given you these gifts, you stir them up within you so that you can be a blessing to those around you.

REFLECTION
Explain in your own words, "anointing comes by association." According to 2 Timothy 1:6, how can you stir up the gifts God has given you?

Imparting health to the sick

The laying on of hands is also associated with the ministry of physical healing. The Lord wants us to be open to His Spirit's prompting, pray for others and have others pray for us to see God's healing power released. The Bible tells us in Mark 16:17-18 that *...these signs will accompany those who believe: In my name...they will place their hands on sick people, and they will get well.* This promise is for every believer. The scriptures tell us that those who believe in Jesus will lay their hands on the sick and they will recover. God has called you and your family to lay hands on those who are sick. For many Christians, the first thing they will do when someone is sick is to call the doctor or go to the drugstore. The first thing we should do when someone is sick is to lay our hands on that person and pray. God tells us that they will recover! The healing power of God goes from one believer to another through the laying on of our hands. There's nothing wrong with going to the doctor, but we need to go to Jesus first.

We read in the book of Acts, chapter 9, that Ananias, who understood the power that is released through the laying on of hands and prayer, laid hands on Saul for healing...*Placing his hands on Saul, he said, "Brother Saul, the Lord—Jesus, who appeared to you on the road as you were coming here—has sent me so that you may see again and be filled with the Holy Spirit." Immediately, something like scales fell from Saul's eyes, and he could see again...(Acts 9:17-18).* Saul had given his life to Jesus Christ on the road to Damascus. Three days later Ananias prayed for Saul, and two things happened. First of all, Saul had been blind for three days, and there were scales on his eyes. The scripture says the scales fell from his eyes when Ananias laid his hands on him and prayed for him. Secondly, Saul was filled with the Holy Spirit.

REFLECTION
What usually happened when Jesus touched people or they touched Him? Can we do the same today?

Jesus constantly imparted health to others as He touched them. We see it in Mark 1:41-42 when Jesus healed a man with leprosy. *Filled with compassion, Jesus reached out his hand and touched the man...Immediately the leprosy left him and he was cured.* We again see Jesus' healing impartation in Mark 6:56. *And wherever he went—into villages, towns or countryside—they placed the sick in the marketplaces. They begged him to let them touch even the edge of his cloak, and all who touched him were healed.*

Jesus lives in each of us today. As we take a step of faith and believe God's Word, we will also be vessels of healing. When we lay our hands on the sick and pray a prayer of faith, the Bible says that they will recover.

Any believer can impart a blessing to another

The laying on of hands is not just for leaders to practice. Every believer can transmit spiritual blessings to others in this way. As God's people, we are the church. When we read the New Testament, we do not see the church as a group of believers who only met together in a building on a Sunday morning; they had interactive relationships with each other daily. They were an integral part of each others' lives. *Every day they continued to meet together in the temple courts. They broke bread in their homes and ate together with glad and sincere hearts, praising God and enjoying the favor of all the people. And the Lord added to their number daily those who were being saved (Acts 2:46-47).*

These believers were experiencing true church. They knew how to impart God's blessing to each other as they related closely together as God's people. The same thing is happening all over the world today. People are getting excited about their relationship with Jesus Christ. People are tired of dead religion. They want the real thing. When Jesus Christ saves them and baptizes them in the Holy Spirit, these believers do not want to just sit around and "play church." They want relationships—with Jesus and with each other! They open up their homes and minister to people right in their own homes.

Small, interactive groups that meet together from house to house and also in larger meetings to receive teaching and experience times of worship are popping up all over the place—cell groups, house churches, fellowship groups, small groups—no matter what you call them, they have the purpose of raising mature Christians and giving every Christian a job to do. Small groups give everyone an opportunity to bless others and impart their lives to others. In small spiritual family groups, the next generation of believers can be nurtured and blessed.

There are times when I feel like I am totally depleted of faith. Since faith comes by hearing the word of God (Romans 10:17), I know that meditating on God's Word is the first step to experiencing renewed faith. But many times I have also been renewed in faith when someone who is "full of faith" prays for me and imparts faith and the healing power of Jesus to me. God has made us in such a way that we need each other. We are His body, and each part of the body is important. When we have a need, the Lord often chooses to use others to impart into our lives what we need. The Lord also wants to use us to impart into others' lives what He has given to us.

REFLECTION
Give some examples of ways the Lord may want to use you to impart spiritual blessings to others.

CHAPTER 2

Imparting Authority

KEY MEMORY VERSE
So after they had fasted and prayed,
they placed their hands on them and sent them off.
Acts 13:3

To acknowledge a specific ministry

Another purpose for the laying on of hands is for publicly acknowledging that someone has received authority from God for a specific ministry and sending them out to fulfill it. The book of Acts 13:2-3 gives an account of the spiritual leaders at the church in Antioch acknowledging and sending out two apostles by laying hands on them. *While they were worshiping the Lord and fasting, the Holy Spirit said, "Set apart for me Barnabas and Saul for the work to which I have called them." So after they had fasted and prayed, they placed their hands on them and sent them off.*

The church leadership imparted to Barnabas and Saul, through the laying on of hands, the blessing and the grace that the Holy Spirit had given them. They were commissioned for a specific ministry which acknowledged the call of God already on their lives. Barnabas and Saul were sent out as one of the most powerful missionary teams that ever walked on the face of the earth!

In Acts, chapter six, a group of men were set apart to distribute food to the widows and to those who were needy. These men were brought before the apostles, who laid their hands on them and imparted to them authority and responsibility for the specific work of food distribution. Because of their history of godliness and faithfulness to the Lord, these "deacons" were set apart for ministry in serving the church in this way. *They chose Stephen, a man full of faith and of the Holy Spirit; also Philip, Procorus, Nicanor, Timon, Parmenas, and Nicolas from Antioch, a convert to Judaism. They presented these men to the apostles, who prayed and laid their hands on them (Acts 6:5-6).*

REFLECTION
Why is it important to receive impartation from leaders before being sent out in a specific ministry?

The scriptures teach us that those who have received authority from God (they already have a proven ministry) should be set apart or consecrated for this specific ministry in the church by the laying on of hands by their church leaders. When I was a young pastor, the spiritual leaders to whom I was accountable laid their hands on me and appointed me to a new role of leadership. The Lord used them to establish this new leadership appointment in my life.

An Old Testament example of imparting authority

An Old Testament example of the laying on of hands for authority in a specific ministry is mentioned in the story of Moses and Joshua. Moses faithfully led the children of Israel in the wilderness. When he came near the end of his ministry, he asked the Lord to appoint a new leader over Israel who would take his place. Joshua, whom Moses had trained for forty years, took his place in leadership among God's people. Let's see what happened during that time of transfer of leadership. We can see clearly the principle of the laying on of hands in Numbers 27:18,20. *So the Lord said to Moses, "Take Joshua son of Nun, a man in whom is the spirit, and lay your hand on him...Give him some of your authority..."*

This happened, of course, when Moses realized the need for Joshua to become the next leader. Joshua already was trained by Moses and called by God, but Moses acknowledged his call by laying hands on Joshua and imparting some of the power and authority that the Lord had given him to lead God's people. Joshua was filled with the spirit of

REFLECTION
Why was it important for Moses to impart his authority to Joshua?

wisdom (Deuteronomy 34:9) after Moses imparted his authority to him. This impartation gave Joshua what Moses had been given. Moses imparted to Joshua the spiritual ability and blessing that he received from the Lord.

Spiritual leaders have the authority to impart

The Bible teaches us that spiritual leaders the Lord places in our lives have been given godly authority and responsibility for us. The Lord commands them to watch out for our souls. Hebrews 13:17 tells us, *Obey your leaders and submit to their authority. They keep watch over you as men who must give an account. Obey them so that their work will be a joy, not a burden, for that would be of no advantage to you.*

First of all, in the body of Christ, we have God's authority because we are sons and daughters of the Lord through faith in Jesus Christ. But as we become involved in the church in areas of ministry, we not only receive authority from God directly, but also receive authority as we are commissioned by the spiritual leaders the Lord has placed in our lives.

In whatever area of service we find ourselves, we would be wise to ask these questions, "Lord, have you placed one or more spiritual leaders in my life who are watching out for my soul?" And the second question to ask is, "Lord, is there someone with whom I can share some of my responsibility?"

When the timing is right, the Lord may ask us to lay our hands on someone else to impart the blessings and spiritual gifts the Lord has given to us.

Spiritual leaders lay their hands on new pastors, leaders and missionaries and commission them to new areas of service. Hands are laid on them to impart the spiritual blessings and gifts that God gives. Something supernatural happens when we lay hands on others and set them apart for a particular ministry. Those who lay their hands on new Christian leaders are responsible to the Lord to "watch out for the souls" of those they are commissioning.

A word of caution: Don't be hasty

DAY 4

A few years ago, I read about a major revival in southeast Asia where a young man came to know Jesus, and God started to use him in a mighty way. The elders of the church came together, laid their hands on him, and prayed, giving him authority and responsibility to be sent out as an evangelist. Nearly everywhere he went, people were saved and healed. The church started to grow and miraculous things happened. After a while, this young man got puffed up with pride and eventually fell into immorality.

When the leaders of the church lovingly confronted him, the young man said, "Look, miracles and healings are happening, who are you to tell me what to do?" He was not willing to be accountable for his actions and refused to repent of his sins. The same leaders, who had laid their hands on this young man a few years earlier commissioning him into this work, informed the young man that they felt responsible.

"Here's what we're going to do," they told him. "We care about you as a person, but we believe your disobedience to the Lord has caused you to misuse the power of God. We are going to pray and receive back that anointing, that empowering that we gave you when we laid hands on you." Do you know what happened? After they had their time of prayer of "decommissioning," the young man no longer received the power of God to heal the sick, and the miracles stopped happening. From that day on, the evangelist did not see the kinds of miracles that he was accustomed to experiencing.

The leaders of the church realized they had laid hands on this young leader giving him responsibility and authority as an evangelist too soon. They learned the hard way what the scripture warns us about in 1 Timothy 5:22. *Do not be hasty in the laying on of hands....*

Church leaders need to be careful not to lay hands on new elders, pastors and ministry leaders prematurely. A person set apart for ministry must have a history of faithfulness to the Lord.

When spiritual leaders lay hands on someone, they stand as God's representatives and give that person authority in Christian service. There is spiritual power released through the laying on of hands when the Lord's people are set apart for specific ministry. In the same way, this authority can be received back.

REFLECTION
Name some valid reasons for refusing to lay hands on someone.

Another word of caution: Keep yourself pure

After 1 Timothy 5:22 mentions that we should not be hasty in laying hands on someone, it continues to say...*and do not share in the sins of others. Keep yourself pure.*

We can "share in" or be a part of another person's sin if we lay hands on him and he has known sin in his life. This verse may be speaking mainly about commissioning someone in the church into specific service, but I believe it can relate to any person for whom we pray.

For example, one evening a young lady in our cell group asked us to pray for her because she was having severe back problems. Someone discerned that she needed to forgive a family member first. When asked about it, she was quick to say she could not forgive the person who had hurt her. We encouraged her to first forgive so she could fully receive the prayer of faith for her healing, which she did. It is important to first pray with others and help them find freedom by confessing their sin, repenting of it, and receiving God's Word and forgiveness before we impart God's blessing or authority to them. Only then will the laying on of hands be truly fruitful.

God wants to use you to lay hands on others to impart His blessing and authority. Everywhere you go, God wants to give you opportunities to impart the authority of God to people. We need, of course, to use wisdom in doing it. For instance, men should minister to men as much as possible. Women need to minister to women. The scriptures seem to imply that older men should be reaching out to younger men, and older women should be reaching out to younger women. Paul gives Titus this guideline, *Likewise, teach the older women...then they can train the younger women...Similarly, encourage the young men...(Titus 2:3-4,6).*

If I'm going to impart the blessing or authority of God to a woman, I will have someone else join me for this time of ministry. We need to use discretion. Proper boundaries should always be maintained between a man and a woman, especially as we lay our hands on them for prayer, so there are no misunderstandings. The scripture tells us to "abstain from all appearance of evil" (1 Thessalonians 5:22).

REFLECTION
Explain in your own words what "abstaining from an appearance of evil" means in the context of laying on of hands.

DAY 6

We have delegated authority to minister to others

The principle of the laying on of hands reminds me of going to the bank. Let's imagine that I go to the bank and take my father's checkbook with a check signed by my father. I would have his delegated authority to get money out of the bank. Let's ask the Lord, "How can I impart Your blessing and authority to people today?" The scriptures tell us that we are priests. We are a royal priesthood, according to 1 Peter 2:9. *But you are a chosen people, a royal priesthood, a holy nation, a people belonging to God, that you may declare the praises of him who called you out of darkness into his wonderful light.* Remember what the priests did in the Old

Testament before Jesus came? They stood between the Lord and His people.

Today, in a new way, we are able to take the blessings of God through the laying on of hands and impart them to people, even to people who aren't yet Christians. The Bible says in 2 Corinthians 3:6 that we are "ministers of the new covenant." You and I are ministers today and can minister to people through the laying on of hands. When they are sick, we minister healing in Jesus' name. When there is a lack of peace, we minister His peace. When they are weak, we minister His strength. When they need to be filled with the Holy Spirit, we minister the precious Holy Spirit.

If you are a part of a small group of believers in a cell group or house church, you know you can do the "work of ministry." You do not have to wait for your cell leader, pastor or elder to pray for others—you can do it yourself. So there are times when you need to go to the hospital to pray for someone who is sick. At a time like this, you should ask the others in your small group to lay hands on you and pray for you. They will impart God's blessing and anointing into your life so that you can be more effective as you pray for the sick and minister in the name of Jesus Christ at the hospital.

If you are a parent, lay your hands on your children and minister to them. You minister the authority of God, the grace of God and the anointing of God to your children through the laying on of hands. I have often had the privilege of imparting His peace, His wisdom, and His strength to people. I have also been privileged to have had many people lay their hands on me and impart these same blessings to me. That is what God wants us to do: minister to one another.

REFLECTION

Give examples of how you have ministered to others through the laying on of hands.

Receiving authority from others

If you are involved in a specific area of ministry, have you ever had someone lay hands on you and commission you into this area of service? Maybe you have a ministry to children in the church or in the community. Receive the Lord's blessing and authority through the laying on of hands. Ask those whom the Lord has placed in your life as spiritual overseers to lay their hands on you and pray for you.

The scriptures tell us in Hebrews 13:7, *Remember your leaders, who spoke the word of God to you. Consider the outcome of their way of life and imitate their faith.* Your spiritual leaders have something you need—you can copy their faith and practices because they are strong in the faith. In doing so, you receive an impartation from them.

Perhaps your local pastor or cell group leader could lay their hands on you and commission you to serve in a particular way. This way you will have God's authority, as well as the authority and blessing of His church to do those things that the Lord has called you to do.

REFLECTION

Have you ever had someone lay hands on you and commission you into an area of service? If not, ask!

CHAPTER 3

We Will Live Forever

KEY MEMORY VERSE

I tell you the truth, whoever hears my word and
believes him who sent me has eternal life
and will not be condemned;
he has crossed over from death to life.
John 5:24

DAY 1

An elementary principle:
The resurrection of the dead

In this chapter, we will examine the important foundation stone of the "resurrection of the dead," and in the next chapter—"eternal judgment." *Therefore, leaving the discussion of the elementary principles of Christ, let us go on to perfection, not laying again the foundation of...resurrection of the dead, and of eternal judgment (Hebrews 6:1-2 NKJ).*

Why is the resurrection of the dead so important to our faith? The difference between Christianity and all other religions is that at the very center of Christianity is this truth: Jesus Christ is alive today! Mohammed is dead. Buddha is dead. All these "great prophets," who founded various world religions, are dead, but Jesus Christ is alive! The early church proclaimed clearly, "Jesus Christ is alive from the dead." It was the foundation of their faith that Jesus Christ had risen from the dead and was alive and well!

The fact of His resurrection is at the center of our faith. He is alive from the dead—this is central to the gospel of Jesus Christ. Jesus was raised from the dead and those who believe in Christ will share His resurrection. We will live forever! In fact, at the end of time, everyone will be resurrected, including the wicked who will be judged and punished. Jesus, Himself, spoke of the resurrection of the dead, both the godly and ungodly, in John 5:28-29. *Do not be amazed at this, for a time is coming when all who are in their graves will hear his voice and come out—those who have done good will rise to live, and those who have done evil will rise to be condemned.*

REFLECTION
What fact is central to the gospel of Jesus Christ? Why is it so important?

DAY 2

Hope arises from knowing we will be resurrected

There is an incredible amount of hope that comes from knowing there will be a resurrection of the dead. For one thing, without eternal life, there are no lasting relationships. Since relationship is so important to God, He created us as eternal beings. He wanted to fellowship with us forever. Christians will have relationships (with

God and each other) throughout eternity because we will live forever!

When Jesus was walking on this earth, His own brother, James, did not realize He was the Son of God (John 7:5) until Jesus arose from the dead and appeared to him. James became an instant believer. Wouldn't you? *...Christ died for our sins according to the Scriptures...he was buried...he was raised on the third day according to the Scriptures...After that, he appeared to James, then to all the apostles (1 Corinthians 15:3,4,7).*

I have gone to many funerals. For those who are true Christians when they die, there is hope. They go on to be with the Lord. Hope surrounds the entire funeral because the resurrection of the dead assures that you will see them again in the future.

Those who don't believe in eternal life have no hope of the future resurrection of the dead. Thomas Paine, known widely by his connection with the American and French revolutions, was also a noted infidel who died miserably in rebellion to the God he turned a deaf ear to. When Christians tried to share with him during his last days on this earth, his response was, "Away with you, and your God too! Leave the room instantly!" Among the last utterances that fell upon the ears of the attendants of this dying infidel, and which have been recorded in history, were the words, "My God, My God, why hast thou forsaken me?" He died without hope.[1]

Everyone lives forever because they are eternal beings. Jesus speaks of a resurrection of life for the believer and a resurrection of judgment for the wicked in John 5:24. *I tell you the truth, whoever hears my word and believes him who sent me has eternal life and will not be condemned; he has crossed over from death to life.*

REFLECTION
Why do Christians have hope? Do you know for sure if you died tonight, you would go to heaven?

Christians will live forever with the Lord, because they have heard God's Word and believed, but unbelievers will be condemned to live in eternal damnation (hell) forever.

---

[1] Compiled by John Myers, *Voices From the Edge of Eternity*, p. 133.

Death is abolished!

The resurrection of Jesus is a triumph over death. Jesus defeated the devil when He rose from the dead. In 1 Corinthians 15:25-26, we read that the last enemy to be abolished is *death*. *For he must reign until he has put all his enemies under his feet. The last enemy to be destroyed is death.*

I have a book in my home that is filled with hundreds of stories telling what happened in the last moments of peoples' lives before death. Some are wonderful stories about Christians who, during the last moments on this earth, catch a glimpse of heaven and peacefully go on to be with the Lord.

However, there are horrible stories told of the end for atheists or agnostics or those who cursed the name of God. Nurses in the same room with these infidels were horrified because these unbelievers were literally seeing the fires of hell before they died.

Friends of ours had their mother living with them for the last years of her life. This elderly Christian woman who loved the Lord with all of her heart, had cataracts in her eyes for years. The day that she passed away and went on to be with the Lord Jesus, the cataracts fell from her eyes. The blue eyes she had in her youth again sparkled. She looked to the corner of her room and reported that she saw Jesus.

While I was in the nation of Zambia, I met a young lady who told an amazing story of heaven. She had just been in a serious car accident and while she was unconscious, she saw a bright light coming into the back of the van. She found herself carried away up into the heavenlies where glorious beings were singing in an angelic language.

REFLECTION
Whom has been defeated because of Jesus' resurrection? How does that affect your life?

As she got closer to the most beautiful place she had ever seen, she began to descend back to the earth. She sensed disappointment when she realized that she was not continuing on toward the glorious city she had seen. The next thing she saw was the top of the bed rails in a hospital room and the voice of a family member saying, "You'll be OK."

"But I want to go on," she told the angelic being at her side.

"It's not your time yet," the angel responded. Then she awoke on the hospital bed. The Lord had given her a small taste of heaven!

Christians have incredible hope because of the resurrection of the dead. When Jesus arose from the dead, he abolished death. We are eternal beings who will live forever with Him.

Our names are in the Book of Life

Did you know the Lord has every believer's name written in a book called the *Book of Life*? When we receive Jesus Christ as the Lord of our lives, our names are entered in His book. He will give us the strength to overcome sin and the temptations of this world until the end. *He who overcomes will, like them, be dressed in white. I will never blot out his name from the book of life, but will acknowledge his name before my Father and his angels (Revelation 3:5).*

Picture this Book of Life containing a complete record of every person's life on electromagnetic recording tape. Modern technology allows an error to be simply and completely erased in a few moments by running the recording head past that particular stretch of tape a second time. There is even a "bulk eraser" which can, in a few seconds, completely erase the whole recorded contents of an entire tape. So it is with the heavenly record of the sinner's life. When a sinner comes for the first time in repentance and faith to Christ, God applies His heavenly "bulk eraser." The whole record of the sinner's former sins is thereby instantly and completely erased, and a clean tape is made available, upon which a new life of faith and righteousness may be recorded. If at any time thereafter the believer should fall again into sin, he needs only to repent and confess his sin, and God erases that particular section of the record, and once again the tape is clean.[1]

When you stand before God, and Jesus Christ is seated at the right hand of the Father, He will say, "I gave my life for you." Your sins have been completely cleansed and taken away,

REFLECTION
Are any of your sins recorded in the Book of Life? Why or why not?

two thousand years ago! That is why I love Jesus Christ so much! He paid the price for my salvation on the cross!

[1] Derek Prince, *Foundation Series*, p. 579.

DAY 5

We graduate to heaven!

When you are saved and come to know Jesus, your spirit is saved. When you die and pass on to eternal life, your spirit goes directly into the presence of Christ in heaven. Immediately, you will be *absent from the body and present with the Lord* (2 Corinthians 5:8 NKJ).

Our resurrected bodies
Romans 8:29
1 Corinthians 15:20,42-44,49
Philippians 3:20-21
1 John 3:2
2 Corinthians 5:7

When Jesus comes again for His people, both those who have died in Christ and the faithful who are still alive are going to receive new, resurrected bodies adapted for heaven. Our spirit, soul, and body will come together at that time into a new resurrected body as we live for God throughout eternity—a body possessing an identity with the body of this life and recognizable (Luke 16:19-31), a body adapted for heaven, free from decay and death (1 Corinthians 15:42), a powerful body not subject to disease (1 Corinthians 15:43), a body not bound by the laws of nature (Luke 24:31; John 20:19; 1 Corinthians 15:44), a body that can eat and drink (Luke 14:15; 22:14-18,30; 24:43). So then, for the Christian, death is like graduation. We are passing on from one phase of life to the next phase of life!

Heaven is going to be a wonderful place. Worshiping God in His presence will be the best experience of all. Just think for a moment about the most wonderful things that you enjoy doing on this earth, and then realize that heaven will be a billion times better than that. Revelation 21:1-4 speaks of heaven. *Then I saw a new heaven and a new earth, for the first heaven and the first earth had passed away, and there was no longer any sea. I saw the Holy City, the new Jerusalem, coming down out of heaven from God, prepared as a bride beautifully dressed for her husband. And I heard a loud voice from the throne saying, "Now the dwelling of God is with men, and he will live with them. They will be his people, and God himself will be with them and be their God. He will wipe every tear from their eyes. There will be no more death or mourning or crying or pain, for the old order of things has passed away."*

REFLECTION
How is death like a graduation? What do you think heaven will be like with a new and perfect body, soul, and spirit?

30   *Biblical Foundations*

Heaven will be a place of total relief. We'll be totally caught up in the presence of God.

Augustus Toplady, author of the immortal song, "Rock of Ages," was dying at age thirty-eight, but he was ready for graduation day. About an hour before he died, he seemed to awaken from a gentle slumber. "Oh, what delights! Who can fathom the joys of the third heaven? What bright sunshine has been spread around me! I have not words to express it. All is light, light, light—the brightness of His glory!" [1]

[1] Compiled by John Myers, *Voices From the Edge of Eternity*, pp. 23,24.

What about children?

Sometimes people ask, "What about children? Are children going to be in heaven?" Yes, heaven will be filled with children! When children are born into this fallen world, they are born with a fallen nature. However, a young child is not old enough to know the difference between God's laws and the cravings of his fallen nature. When a child comes to the "age of accountability," he has to make the decision to choose right from wrong. He eventually chooses God or chooses his own way which would lead to eternal separation from God.

Children are without guilt and spiritual accountability until they sin against God's law. *Once I was alive apart from law; but when the commandment came, sin sprang to life and I died (Romans 7:9).* Paul says he was "once alive apart from the law," showing us that a child is "alive" until he understands the difference between right and wrong. Only God knows when that time is. However, after a child knows the law, then sin revives and they

REFLECTION
What happens to babies when they die?
What qualifies a person for entrance to heaven, according to Matthew 18:3?

die. In other words, when we come to the realization that we are sinning against the law of God, we are spiritually dead. That is why we need to give our lives to Jesus Christ. We need to be born again.

Each of our four children were convicted of their sins at a young age and received Jesus Christ as their Lord and Savior. When they were babies, they had no understanding of conviction of sin. However, the day came (their "age of accountability") for each of them to respond to the Holy Spirit's conviction.

Every person must come to a place of decision and respond to Jesus Christ and His offer of salvation in order to secure their place in heaven. Jesus said in Matthew 18:3, *Assuredly, I say to you, unless you are converted and become as little children, you will by no means enter the kingdom of heaven.*

Preparing a place for us

At this very moment, the Lord is preparing a place for us to live throughout all of eternity. Jesus tells us in His Word, *Do not let your hearts be troubled. Trust in God; trust also in me. In my Father's house are many rooms; if it were not so, I would have told you. I am going there to prepare a place for you. And if I go and prepare a place for you, I will come back and take you to be with me that you also may be where I am (John 14:1-3).*

Can you imagine it! Jesus is preparing a special place just for you in heaven! Jesus Christ is coming back for us! Those of us who are still alive on this earth when He returns will meet Him in the air. Those who are dead, whose spirits are with the Lord, will return with the Lord and He will give them new bodies. It is going to be an exciting day! *Brothers, we do not want you to be ignorant about those who fall asleep, or to grieve like the rest of men, who have no hope. We believe that Jesus died and rose again and so we believe that God will bring with Jesus those who have fallen asleep in him. According to the Lord's own word, we tell you that we who are still alive, who are left till the coming of the Lord, will certainly not precede those who have fallen asleep. For the Lord himself will come down from heaven, with a loud command, with the voice of the archangel and with the trumpet call of God, and the dead in Christ will rise first. After that, we who are still alive and are left will be caught up together with them in the clouds to meet the Lord in the air. And so we will be with the Lord forever (1 Thessalonians 4:13-17).*

Jesus Christ is coming back for His church—His people. It is going to be the most historic event since His visit to this planet two thousand years ago. As Christians, we should live each day as if He is coming today! If He doesn't come back for a few years yet, that's okay. We will just keep looking up, expecting His return, as we live in fellowship with the Holy Spirit each day.

Biblical Foundations

D. L. Moody, an evangelist from the nineteenth century, knew a place was being prepared for him in heaven. On his deathbed, he seemed to see beyond the veil as he exclaimed, "Earth recedes, heaven opens before me. It is beautiful. If this is death, it is sweet. There is no valley here. God is calling me, and I must go. This is my triumph; this is my coronation day! I have been looking forward to it for years." [1]

[1] Compiled by John Myers, *Voices From the Edge of Eternity*, pp. 23, 24.

CHAPTER 4

God
Judges All

KEY MEMORY VERSE
Just as man is destined to die once,
and after that to face judgment.
Hebrews 9:27

An elementary principle: Eternal judgment

In the previous chapter, we examined the principle of the "resurrection of the dead." In this chapter, we will look at another basic foundation stone of the Christian faith that is linked to the resurrection of the dead—"eternal judgment." *Therefore, leaving the discussion of the elementary principles of Christ, let us go on to perfection, not laying again the foundation of...eternal judgment (Hebrews 6:1-2 NKJ).*

What is judgment? The word *judgment* literally means *verdict.* When a judge sentences someone, he passes the verdict. Judgment is pronounced. There is no reversal. The scripture says that judgment is eternal. Eternal judgment is a verdict given that will last forever.

What is eternity? Imagine one little bird coming to the seashore every one thousand years. This bird then takes one grain of sand and carries it from the seashore and drops it somewhere into the ocean. After all of the sand on all of the seashores along all of the oceans of the world would be totally depleted of sand, eternity would have just begun! It is *that* hard to fathom the length of eternity!

Every man and woman who has ever lived will someday be judged by God for all of eternity. *Just as man is destined to die once, and after that to face judgment (Hebrews 9:27).* The faithful do not need to fear God's judgment because they will receive eternal life in heaven with Jesus. The wicked, however will be eternally punished. *Then they will go away to eternal punishment, but the righteous to eternal life (Matthew 25:46).*

Voltaire was a noted French infidel who spent most of his life ridiculing Christianity. When Voltaire had a stroke which he realized would terminate his life, he was terrified and tortured with such agony that at times he gnashed his teeth in rage against God and man. At other times, he would plead, "O Christ! I must die—abandoned of God and of

REFLECTION
What is eternal judgment? Where do the wicked go and where do the righteous go, according to Matthew 25:46?

men!" Voltaire's infidel associates were afraid to approach his bedside. His nurse repeatedly said that for all the wealth of Europe she would never want to see another infidel die. It was a scene of horror that lies beyond all exaggeration.[1]

While heaven is a place of unimaginable beauty where God's people will fellowship with each other and their God forever, hell is a place of endless suffering and punishment for those who reject Christ.

[1] Compiled by John Myers, *Voices From the Edge of Eternity*, p. 22.

The judgment seat of Christ

Someday we will all stand before the living God in judgment. For believers in Jesus Christ, our sins were judged on the cross two thousand years ago, so it will not be a judgment of condemnation. However, those who have not received the Lord Jesus Christ into their lives will await sentencing. There is no escape. *For we must all appear before the judgment seat of Christ, that each one may receive what is due him for the things done while in the body, whether good or bad. Since, then, we know what it is to fear the Lord, we try to persuade men...(2 Corinthians 5:10-11).*

Now is the time to tell people the good news that will set men and women free. Today, as I write this, I had the privilege of assisting a young couple as they gave their lives to Jesus Christ. Because of their decision for Christ, their sins are forgiven and they will not have to face eternal punishment. They will live forever in God's kingdom!

Praise God for Jesus, who paid the price on the cross to save us from eternal damnation! When we receive Jesus as Lord, He says, "I love you, I will cleanse you, and I will make you a brand new person, as a part of My family. You will live with Me forever." It is God's plan for us to be saved. *For God did not send his Son into the world to condemn the world, but to save the world through him (John 3:17).*

REFLECTION
Imagine standing before God on judgment day. How can you be sure you will gain eternal life?

Christians will have to give an account at judgment

Although believers are free of God's judgment of condemnation and will go to heaven, the Bible does say we will have to give an account as to the degree of our faithfulness to God, according to 1 Corinthians 3:12-15. *If any man builds on this foundation using gold, silver, costly stones, wood, hay or straw, his work will be shown for what it is, because the Day will bring it to light. It will be revealed with fire, and the fire will test the quality of each man's work. If what he has built survives, he will receive his reward. If it is burned up, he will suffer loss; he himself will be saved, but only as one escaping through the flames.*

On that Day, at the judgment seat of Christ, God will examine openly our character, secret acts, good deeds, motives, attitudes, etc. If we have not lived holy and godly lives and shown mercy and kindness, our foundation is weak—one of "wood, hay or stubble, rather than gold, silver, or precious stones." Although we will receive salvation, we will experience great "loss." A careless believer suffers loss in the following ways: by feeling shame at Christ's coming (1 John 2:28), loss of his life's work for God (1 Corinthians 3:13-15), loss of glory and honor before God (Romans 2:7), loss of opportunity for service and authority in heaven (Matthew 25:14-30; 5:15; 19:30) and loss of rewards (1 Corinthians 3:12-14; Philippians 3:14; 2 Timothy 4:8).

When our attitude and motivation reflects the fruit of the Spirit and a Christ-like love, our works will be built with precious stones with many rewards from God. If we are motivated more by selfish ambition than by the leading of God's Holy Spirit, those works will be destroyed—burned up. These solemn words should motivate us to live faithful, self-sacrificing lives for the Lord.

A well-known Bible teacher who has spent dozens of years proclaiming the gospel throughout the world writes the following to describe the moment when God will judge every Christian's works: "In the fiery rays of those eyes, as each one stands before His judgment seat, all that is base, insincere and valueless in His people's works will be instantly and eternally consumed. Only that which is of true and enduring value will survive, purified and refined by fire. As we consider this scene of judgment, each of us needs to ask himself: How may I serve Christ in this life, so that my works will stand the test of fire in that day?"[1]

REFLECTION
What will be "brought to light" in a believer's life on judgment day according to 1 Corinthians 3:12-15?

[1] Derek Prince, *Foundation Series,* p. 583.

The judgment of the wicked—a literal hell

Although everyone, living or dead, throughout the ages will be judged, the Bible portrays a different picture of the final destiny of the lost as they stand before the living God. Revelation 20:11-15 says, *Then I saw a great white throne and him who was seated on it. Earth and sky fled from his presence, and there was no place for them. And I saw the dead, great and small, standing before the throne, and books were opened. Another book was opened, which is the book of life. The dead were judged according to what they had done as recorded in the books. The sea gave up the dead that were in it, and death and Hades gave up the dead that were in them, and each person was judged according to what he had done. Then death and Hades were thrown into the lake of fire. The lake of fire is the second death. If anyone's name was not found written in the book of life, he was thrown into the lake of fire.*

> **Hell, the final destiny of the lost**
> Romans 2:9; Matthew 13:42,50; 22:13
> 25:30,46; Mark 9:43; 19:20; 14:11
> 2 Thessalonians 1:9; 2 Peter 2:4
> Hebrews 10:31

What is the *second death* mentioned here? The *second death* is an eternal hell that burns with fire for ever and ever. This terrible picture of hell is almost too horrible to think about, but according to the Bible, there is a real, burning hell. The scriptures tell us, *The Son of Man will send out his angels, and they will weed out of his kingdom everything that causes sin and all who do evil. They will throw them into the fiery furnace, where there will be weeping and gnashing of teeth. Then the righteous will shine like the sun in the kingdom of their Father. He who has ears, let him hear (Matthew 13:41-43).*

The destinies of both the Christian and the unbeliever are irreversible at death. In Luke 16:19-31, we read the story of the rich man and Lazarus. The rich man spent his life consumed in self-centered living and found himself in hell after he died. Lazarus was a beggar, a poor man who lived in the rich man's neighborhood, and was fed by the crumbs that came from the rich man's table. His

REFLECTION
If a person's name is not found in the Book of Life, what is his final destiny, according to Revelation 20:11-15? Is this destiny reversible (see Luke 16:19-31)?

heart was right with God, and when he died, he was immediately taken to paradise. The rich man cried out because of his torment in hell, but it was too late.

Some people say sarcastically, "I'm not afraid of hell. I'll just be having a party with all my friends." Hell will not be a party. It will be an eternal fire—a place of horrible torment.

Hell is prepared for the devil and his angels

Jesus did not make hell for people. He made hell for the devil and his angels. *Then he will say to those on his left, "Depart from me, you who are cursed, into the eternal fire prepared for the devil and his angels" (Matthew 25:41).*

The worst thing about hell is the lack of the goodness of God. Everything good that we know of is from God. Can you imagine being in a place where there is nothing good? That is what hell is going to be like, in the midst of all the torment from the fires of hell.

Just like there are degrees of reward in heaven, there are degrees of punishment in hell, according to the Bible. *That servant who knows his master's will and does not get ready or does not do what his master wants will be beaten with many blows. But the one who does not know and does things deserving punishment will be beaten with few blows. From everyone who has been given much, much will be demanded; and from the one who has been entrusted with much, much more will be asked (Luke 12:47-48).*

In other words, those persons who have heard the gospel and know about the Truth (Jesus), and simply continue to turn away from Him, are under a much worse judgment than those who have never heard. I used to think that the people who have been involved in all kinds of "gross sin"—like murder, adultery and witchcraft—would have the worst punishment in hell. However, here the Bible tells us that people who know the truth and do not obey will have a stricter punishment in hell than those who didn't know or obey. The sobering truth, however, is that hell is

REFLECTION
Did God create hell for bad people. What is hell like, according to Mark 9:43?

hell. Whether it is a million degrees or ten million degrees, it is hell—a "fire that never goes out" (Mark 9:43), a place of endless torment and pain, a terrifying reality for those condemned.

What about people who have never heard of Jesus?

Jesus Christ is the only way that we can get to God and live eternally with Him. Jesus, Himself, said in John 14:6...*I am the way and the truth and the life. No one comes to the Father except through me.*

So what about people who have never heard of Jesus Christ? We can be assured that God is a fair judge. The Bible says He is righteous (1 John 2:1). When someone questions the fairness of God's judgment concerning those who have not heard, my initial response often is, "But *you* have heard; what is *your* response to Jesus?" Romans 2:14-15 says, *Indeed, when Gentiles, who do not have the law, do by nature things required by the law, they are a law for themselves, even though they do not have the law, since they show that the requirements of the law are written on their hearts, their consciences also bearing witness, and their thoughts now accusing, now even defending them.*

REFLECTION
How will God be a fair judge, according to Romans 2:14-15?

Here we see that the Lord judges according to what someone has learned, what their conscience tells them. Everyone has a measure of knowledge of right and wrong, and we need to trust God to be a fair judge. God is a faithful and just God (1 John 1:9). He is more fair than any human being could ever be. It is those of us who *do* know the truth of Jesus Christ that have no excuse. Galatians 6:7-8 says, *Do not be deceived: God cannot be mocked. A man reaps what he sows. The one who sows to please his sinful nature, from that nature will reap destruction; the one who sows to please the Spirit, from the Spirit will reap eternal life.*

That is why we need to sow into our lives spiritually. We must read and meditate on the Word of God, and share its truth with others. We need to develop an intimate relationship with our Lord Jesus. Whatever we sow spiritually, we will reap spiritually. Whenever we sow from the flesh (our own evil nature), we will reap that kind of eternal destiny. Let's sow to the Spirit, and live for Him throughout all of eternity. *But seek first his kingdom and his righteousness, and all these things will be given to you as well (Matthew 6:33).*

What *things*, you ask? All the blessings of God including eternal life in heaven. People live forever. What is the kingdom of God? It is God and His people. It's a relationship with God and relationships with one another that will last forever.

We must tell them the Good News

An atheist in England made a statement that I never forgot. He said, "I am an atheist, because if I believed what Christians preach, I would crawl on my hands and knees on broken glass to tell one person how he could escape the punishment of which they speak." Christians know that Christianity is real and an eternal destiny awaits both the saved and the unsaved.

Back in the early days of our church, God gave a vision to a young man: "I saw in my vision the fires of hell. And I saw many, many people walking toward the fires of hell, falling over the cliff into hell. Then I saw another group of people, an army. I saw people joining together hand in hand, and they were going down to the brink of the fire and pulling people up at the last moment before they went plunging over. People were being literally snatched from hell. That is what God has called us to do as a church." We need to do whatever we can to see people snatched from the fires of hell to live for God eternally.

When Christians see themselves as spiritual soldiers in His army, we will be motivated to pull people out of the fires of hell because we know the truth that will set them free. The truth will set those free who respond to the name of Jesus.

Jesus Christ is coming back soon. We have a job to do! Jesus admonished believers to remember all the lost souls that will spend eternity in hell if the gospel is not presented to them. The fields are ready and white for harvest now, and we must tell them the good news. Jesus said, *Do you not say, "Four months more and then the harvest"? I tell you, open your eyes and look at the fields! They are ripe for harvest (John 4:35b).*

REFLECTION
How can you snatch someone from the brink of hell? Have you ever done this?

The reality of an eternal judgment should cause all believers to hate sin and diligently seek the lost to tell them of God's wonderful plan for mankind.

People who joke about hell have no idea how real hell will be. After an individual dies there will be no more opportunity to escape (Hebrews 9:27). There is an old saying, "The road to hell is paved with good intentions." If you have not done so already, now is the time to accept God's provision of His Son, Jesus Christ, for you to live forever! Don't delay.

Imparting Blessing and Healing

1. **An elementary principle: The laying on of hands**
   a. Laying on of hands (Hebrews 6:1-2).
   b. A supernatural transference (Leviticus 16:21-22) as when Aaron laid his hands on a goat and confessed the people's sins.
   c. An impartation of power and blessing is transferred from one person to another through the laying on of hands. It imparts healing, spiritual gifts and authority.

2. **Imparting life to one another**
   a. There is tremendous power in our lives to bless: Jesus blessed the children (Mark 10:16).
   b. The Lord wants us to bless others so we can inherit a blessing (1 Peter 3:8-9).

3. **Imparting the power of the Holy Spirit**
   a. There are specific purposes for the laying on of hands in the Old and New Testaments.
   b. The laying on of hands is for imparting to those seeking the baptism in the Holy Spirit (Acts 8:14-15; 17).

4. **Imparting spiritual gifts**
   a. Laying on of hands is for imparting spiritual gifts. Romans 1:11-12
   b. Nine spiritual gifts (1 Corinthians 12:8-10) we can impart to others through the laying on of hands. More gifts to impart (Romans 12:6-8).

5. Associate with those who can impart gifts to you

a. Leaders of early church laid hands on Timothy to impart spiritual gifts he needed (1 Timothy 4:14).

b. Timothy was encouraged to stir up the gift (1 Timothy 1:6).

c. How can you stir up the gifts God's given you?

6. Imparting health to the sick

a. Believers can lay hands on the sick and they will recover. Mark 16:17-18

b. Ananias laid hands on Saul for healing (Acts 9:17-18).

c. What happened when Jesus touched people (Mark 6:56)?

7. Any believer can impart a blessing to another

a. As God's people, we are the church. Believers should have interactive relationships with each other just as they did in the early church (Acts 2:46-47).

b. Fellow believers in small groups can easily impart blessings to each other, thus encouraging each other. Give examples of how you have imparted a spiritual blessing to another.

Imparting Authority

1. To acknowledge a specific ministry

   a. Church at Antioch laid hands on two apostles thereby acknowledging they had received authority from God for their specific ministry (Acts 13:2-3).

   b. Authority and responsibility imparted to deacons. Acts 6:5-6

   c. Those who have a proven ministry should be set aside for this ministry in the church by the laying on of hands. Why is this important?

2. An Old Testament example of imparting authority

   a. Moses gives his authority to Joshua (Numbers 27:18,20).

   b. Why was it important for Moses to impart his authority to Joshua?

3. Spiritual leaders have the authority to impart

   a. Spiritual leaders watch out for us (Hebrews 13:17).

   b. We receive authority as we are commissioned by our spiritual leaders to an area of service.

4. A word of caution: Don't be hasty

   Ex: A young evangelist was given spiritual authority, but became prideful and fell into sin.

   a. A person should have a history of faithfulness to the Lord before he is set apart for ministry.

   b. Spiritual leaders should be careful about laying hands on someone to stand as God's representative too soon. 1 Timothy 5:22a

5. **Another word of caution: Keep yourself pure**
   a. We can "share in" someone's sin if they have known sin in their lives and we lay hands on them (1 Timothy 5:22).
   b. Men minister to men, women to women as much as possible (Titus 2:3-6,6).

6. **We have delegated authority to minister to others**
   a. We are priests (1 Peter 2:9).
   b. We are ministers of the new covenant (2 Corinthians 3:6) and can minister through the laying on of hands.
   c. We have delegated authority from the Lord to minister to others.

7. **Receiving authority from others**
   a. Receive the Lord's blessing and authority to minister.
   b. Have a spiritual leader commission you into a particular area of service (Hebrews 13:7).
   c. Your spiritual leaders have something you need. You can "imitate their faith."

We Will Live Forever

1. **An elementary principle: The resurrection of the dead**
   a. The foundation of Christianity is that Jesus rose from the dead (Hebrews 6:1-2) and we will share in His resurrection.
   b. We are eternal beings who will live forever!
   c. Jesus spoke of this resurrection (John 5:28-29).

2. **Hope arises from knowing we will be resurrected**
   a. Without eternal life, there are no lasting relationships.
   b. James, Jesus' brother, realized after Jesus rose from the dead that He was really the Son of God.
   1 Corinthians 15:3,4,7
   c. At funerals of Christians, there is hope.
   Ex: Unbelievers like Thomas Paine die without hope.
   d. Resurrection of life for the believer and resurrection of judgment for the wicked (John 5:24).

3. **Death is abolished!**
   a. The resurrection of Jesus is a triumph over death.
   b. The last enemy to be destroyed is death
   1 Corinthians 15:25-26
   Ex: Difference between stories of those who die with hope or without hope.
   c. Christians have incredible hope because of the resurrection of the dead.

4. Our names are in the Book of Life
a. When we receive Jesus, our names go in the Book of Life. Revelation 3:5
b. This book contains a complete record of every person's life, but a "bulk eraser" erases our past when we come in repentance to Jesus.

5. We graduate to heaven!
a. When you die, your spirit goes directly to heaven. 2 Corinthians 5:8
b. We will receive new, resurrected bodies in heaven.
c. Death is like graduation, passing from one phase of life to the next.
d. Description of heaven (Revelation 21:1-4).

6. What about children?
a. Children are without guilt and spiritual accountability until they sin against God (Romans 7:9).
b. Only God knows when that time of accountability is for each individual.
c. All must "become as little children" to enter the kingdom of heaven (Matthew 18:3).

7. Preparing a place for us
a. Jesus is preparing a place for us to live throughout eternity. John 14:1-3
b. Jesus is coming back for His church—His people. 1 Thessalonians 4:13-17
c. We should live each day as if He is coming today!

God Judges All

1. An elementary principle: Eternal judgment
Hebrews 6:1-2

a. Judgment means verdict. Eternal judgment is a verdict that will last forever.

b. Eternity very hard to fathom.

c. Every person faces judgment (Hebrews 9:27).

d. Faithful do not fear judgment but the wicked will be eternally punished (Matthew 25:46).

e. Hell is a place of endless suffering. Heaven is a place of unimaginable beauty.

2. The judgment seat of Christ

a. We must all appear before the judgment seat of Christ.

b. For the Christian, it is not a judgment of condemnation.

c. Now is the time to tell people the good news before it is too late (2 Corinthians 5:10-11).

d. God's plan is for us to be saved (John 3:17).

3. Christians will have to give an account at judgment

a. Christians are free of judgment, but will have to give an account as to their faithfulness to God.
1 Corinthians 3:12-15

b. If we have not lived holy lives, we experience "loss."

c. If our attitudes reflect the fruit of the Spirit, our works are built with precious stones and many rewards from God. If not, those works are burned up.

4. The judgment of the wicked—a literal hell
a. The final destiny of the lost: hell (Revelation 20:11-15).
b. Hell is described in Matthew 13:41-43 as a place of horrible torment.
c. The destinies of both Christian and non-Christian are irreversible at death.
   Luke 16:19-31: story of rich man and Lazarus.

5. Hell is prepared for the devil and his angels
a. Jesus made hell for the devil, not people (Matthew 25:41).
b. There will be degrees of punishment in hell (Luke 12:47-48).
c. Persons who heard the gospel and rejected it are under worse judgment than those who never heard.
d. Still, hell is hell—a fire that never goes out (Mark 9:43).

6. What about people who have never heard of Jesus?
a. Jesus is the only way to God (John 14:6).
b. God is a fair, righteous judge (1 John 2:1).
c. The Lord judges according to what someone has learned, what their conscience tells them (Romans 2:14-15).

7. We must tell them the Good News
a. Christians need to do whatever we can to see people snatched from the fires of hell.
   Ex: Vision of plucking people from hell.
b. We are soldiers in God's army and have a job to do.
c. The fields are ripe for harvest (John 4:35).
d. Hell is no joke. After death, there is no longer an opportunity to escape hell (Hebrews 9:27). Accept God's provision of Jesus Christ, and live forever with Him!

Chapter 1
Imparting Blessing and Healing
Journaling space for reflection questions

DAY 1 *What is supernatural about the laying on of hands? Have you ever asked another Christian to impart a blessing to you by the laying on of hands? Describe what you asked for.*

DAY 2 *How does the Lord impart a blessing to us and through us?*

DAY 3 *Can you receive the Holy Spirit without the laying on of hands? Has God used you to impart the Holy Spirit to someone through the laying on of hands? Describe.*

DAY 4 List the nine spiritual gifts found in 1 Corinthians 12. List seven more spiritual gifts found in Romans 12. Do you have any of these gifts? Have you imparted any of them to others?

DAY 5 Explain in your own words, "anointing comes by association." According to 2 Timothy 1:6, how can you stir up the gifts God has given you?

DAY 6 What usually happened when Jesus touched people or they touched Him? Can we do the same today?

DAY 7 Give some examples of ways the Lord may want to use you to impart spiritual blessings to others.

Chapter 2
Imparting Authority
Journaling space for reflection questions

DAY 1 *Why is it important to receive impartation from leaders before being sent out in a specific ministry?*

DAY 2 *Why was it important for Moses to impart his authority to Joshua?*

DAY 3 *Do you desire to have someone lay hands on you to impart a blessing and spiritual gifts? Ask!*

DAY 4 *Name some valid reasons for refusing to lay hands on someone.*

DAY 5 *Explain in your own words what "abstaining from an appearance of evil" means in the context of laying on of hands.*

DAY 6 *Give examples of how you have ministered to others through the laying on of hands.*

DAY 7 *Have you ever had someone lay hands on you and commission you into an area of service? If not, ask!*

Chapter 3
We Will Live Forever
Journaling space for reflection questions

What fact is central to the gospel of Jesus Christ?
Why is it so important?

Why do Christians have hope? Do you know for sure if you died tonight, you would go to heaven?

Whom has been defeated because of Jesus' resurrection? How does that affect your life?

DAY 4

Are any of your sins recorded in the Book of Life?
Why or why not?

DAY 5

How is death like a graduation? What do you think heaven will be like with a new and perfect body, soul, and spirit?

DAY 6

What happens to babies when they die? What qualifies a person for entrance to heaven, according to Matthew 18:3?

DAY 7

What is Jesus preparing for us, according to John 14:1-3?
When is Jesus coming back for us?

Chapter 4
God Judges All
Journaling space for reflection questions

DAY 1 *What is eternal judgment? Where do the wicked go and where do the righteous go, according to Matthew 25:46?*

DAY 2 *Imagine standing before God on judgment day. How can you be sure you will gain eternal life?*

DAY 3 *What will be "brought to light" in a believer's life on judgment day according to 1 Corinthians 3:12-15?*

If a person's name is not found in the Book of Life, what is his
final destiny, according to Revelation 20:11-15?
Is this destiny reversible (see Luke 16:19-31)?

Did God create hell for bad people?
What is hell like, according to Mark 9:43?

How will God be a fair judge, according to Romans 2:14-15?

How can you snatch someone from the brink of hell?
Have you ever done this?

Daily Devotional Extra Days

If you are using this book as a daily devotional, you will notice there are 28 days in this study. Depending on the month, you may need the three extra days' studies given here.

Being Changed

DAY 29

Read 1 Corinthians 15:51-52. How quickly will you be changed when Jesus comes again? How can you know this will be? What must you do to be prepared?

The Righteous

DAY 30

Read Matthew 13:37-43. What will the angels gather out of His kingdom to cast into the furnace of fire? What will the righteous do? Who are the righteous?

Redeemed

DAY 31

Read Isaiah 43:25;44:22. How does God see you when He looks at you? Why? Is your life a reflection of your gratitude to God for redeeming you from hell? What can you do to thank Him?

Coordinates with this series!

Biblical Foundations for Children

Creative learning experiences for ages 4-12, patterned after the *Biblical Foundation Series*, with truths in each lesson. Takes kids on the first steps in their Christian walk by teaching them how to build solid foundations in their young lives. by Jane Nicholas, 176 pages: $17.95 ISBN:1-886973-35-0

Other books by Larry Kreider

House to House

The church is waking up to the simple, successful house to house strategy practiced by the New Testament church. *House to House* documents how God called a small fellowship of believers to become a house to house movement. During the past years, DOVE Christian Fellowship Int'l has grown into a family of cell-based churches and house churches networking throughout the world. by Larry Kreider, 206 pages: $8.95 ISBN:1-880828-81-2

The Cry for Spiritual Fathers & Mothers

Returning to the biblical truth of spiritual parenting so believers are not left fatherless and disconnected. How loving, seasoned spiritual fathers and mothers help spiritual children reach their full potential in Christ. by Larry Kreider, 186 pages: $11.95 ISBN:1-886973-42-3

Helping You Build Cell Churches

A complete biblical blueprint for small group ministry, this comprehensive manual covers 54 topics! Gives full, integrated training to build cell churches from the ground up. Compiled by Brian Sauder and Larry Kreider, 256 pages: $19.95 ISBN:1-886973-38-5

Check our Web site:
www.dcfi.org

63

Spiritual Fathering & Mothering Seminar

Practical preparation for believers who want to have and become spiritual parents. Includes a manual and the book *The Cry For Spiritual Fathers & Mothers*.

Effective Small Group Ministry Seminar

Developing strategy for successful cell groups. For cell leaders and pastors. Includes a *House To House* book and a seminar manual.

Youth Cell Ministry Seminar

Learn the values behind youth cells so cell ministry does not become just another program at your church. For adult and teen leaders!

New House Church Networks Seminar

Learn how new house churches (micro-churches) are started, kept from pitfalls, and work with the rest of the body of Christ.

Elder's Training Seminar

Based on New Testament leadership principles, this seminar will equip elders to provide protection, direction and correction in the local church. Includes *The Biblical Role of Elders in Today's Church* book and a manual.

Church Planting Clinic

Designed to help you formulate a successful strategy for cell-based church planting. For those involved in church planting and those considering it. Includes a *Helping You Build Cell Churches* Manual.

Counseling Basics Seminar for Small Group Leaders

This seminar takes you through the basics of counseling, specifically in small group ministry. Includes a comprehensive manual.

Fivefold Ministry Seminar

A seminar designed to release healthy, effective fivefold ministry in the local church. Includes a *Helping You Build Cell Churches* Manual.

Marriage Mentoring Training Seminar

Trains church leaders and mature believers to help prepare engaged couples for a strong marriage foundation by using the mentoring format of *Called Together*. Includes a *Called Together* Manual.

Seminars held at various locations throughout the US and Canada. For complete brochures and upcoming dates:

Call 1-800-848-5892

www.dcfi.org   email: info@dcfi.org